ACKNOWLEDGEMENTS are due to the editors of *Cross-Currents*, *Counter-Currents*, *Envoi*, *Flint*, *Home and Away* and *South*, in whose pages some of these poems first appeared, also to Toni Savage of Leicester and Graham Williams of The Florin Press in Kent, who first printed some of them.

'Heartsease' won 2nd prize in the *Hampshire County Library/Radio Solent Poetry Competition* 1990, and has been broadcast on Radio Solent; 'Pot-Pourri' and the 'Ballad of Brighton Beach' were jointly awarded the Poetry Trophy at the *Southampton Writers' Conference* in 1986, as was 'Harlequinade' in 1990; 'Kitchen Cantata' won 1st prize in the *Envoi Sonnet Competition* 1988.

This volume was published with assistance from the Ralph Lewis Award at the University of Sussex.

Supported by

Cornwall
County Council

WITH THE ASSISTANCE OF

SOUTH WEST ARTS

Recipient of an Arts Council Incentive Funding Award

In memory of my sister

Janet Bewick, 1911-1991

and our joint gift

to R.

Of the many people from whom I have received friendly and helpful criticism and support in the writing of these poems, I would particularly like to thank my sister Janet and my friend Physhe Wright, also Jeremy Hooker, Kevin Crossley-Holland, Kay Cotton and all members of the Winchester Poetry Workshop and Wykeham Poets. To Lorraine Curtis especial thanks for many hours of patient work on her word processor.

HEARTSEASE

Heartsease

ELIZABETH BEWICK

PETERLOO POETS

First published in 1991
by Peterloo Poets
2 Kelly Gardens, Calstock, Cornwall PL18 9SA, U.K.

**A catalogue record for this book is available
from the British Library**

ISBN 1–871471–24–9

Printed in Great Britain by
Latimer Trend & Company Ltd, Plymouth

Contents

"Heartsease, Wild Pansy, Monkey-faces, Three-faces-under-a-hood, Stepmothers, Love-in-idleness, Trinities.

Heartsease is adept at protecting itself from bad weather by drooping its head at night or at the onset of rain, so that its petals stay dry. It was formerly used as a remedy for epilepsy and diseases of the heart, and this probably accounts for its mediaeval name. It was Christianised in the sixteenth century, to become Trinities or Three-faces-under-a-hood.

This is the flower that Puck gave Oberon to work the mischief of *A Midsummer Night's Dream*, and it was often a vital ingredient in love-charms. The dried plant was powdered and put into the food or hidden in the room of the person desired. It is the food plant of the gorgeous butterfly Queen of Spain Fritillary, *Issoria lathonia*."

(from *The Wild Garden* by Lys de Bray, Weidenfeld and Nicholson, 1978)

Heartsease

A warm night after rain, I step outside
and smell the new-washed air that emanates
from roses in the gardens of the town
and from the bedrooms where the young girls lie
wakeful in tented sheets, their hearts aflame
for lovers in their still undreamt-of dreams.
Another shower sends me back indoors
to my own garden mirrored in the rain;
I close the window in a sudden chill
and drink my cocoa in a spindrift shawl.

Morning again, and pansies barely dry
are little battered flags of brilliance
growing in cracks between my paving stones.
Heartsease, you called them, and for love of you
I touch their petals with a gentle hand
and pick the weathered dead-heads carefully.

My garden is a meadow lush with weeds
in whose green depths such hidden flowers grow
as one day will suffice for all your needs.
I thought so once, sadly uncertain now
I cherish flowers that thrived on my neglect
and throw the weeds upon the rising heap.
Yet, in my seventieth year, I am ashamed
because of all the things I have not done,
the sins committed in my carelessness;
you told me once my greatest talent was
simply for loving, now I need to know
that heartsease pansies still have power to heal.

Art Deco

for Jeremy Hooker

Scratching at paint
through a week of turning hours,
spreading white over cream
to cover old scars.

Dissecting thought,
scraping the surface of days
with a strident sound,
the knife on the glass.

Always the tune,
discordant at times, but true
to the rhythm of life,
the blade in its sheath.

The question unasked
that lies at the edge of the mind
unanswered in turn,
will it come to light?

The careful gloss
put on with a shaking hand,
how long will it last
and lasting, look right?

The Need for Dark

Be wary of the light
at onset of old age,
we need the dark for dreams.

Street lamp's intrusive stare
nags all night in a room
to keep the mind awake.

Restless, I pick old scabs
to find them wet with blood,
my thoughts twist in the light.

Lost images emerge:
I rocked you in my womb,
what gives you comfort now?

The blessed dark, you said,
and turned aside to sleep
sure of my watchful care.

I hang new blinds to shield
the windows of your dream,
my eyes turn from the dawn.

Waiting for Godot

Forget-me-nots
that grow unbidden on the lawn
spoil the green symmetry.
I pull them out
pause, then try fruitlessly
to push them back again, till—
awkward in a new distress—
I ram them
in my best vase.

Pink helianthemum
opens in the sun,
bright petals spilling
on the blue-black edge
of renovated pond;
replanted lilies float,
and water weed,
green and mysterious,
sends out long fingers to assess the air.

I scrub two garden chairs
and stand them
side by side.
They stare whitely back at me,
waiting for Godot
in a desolation more complete
than if I had not tried
to cover up
the wilderness.

My Face to the Sea

My face to the sea
I walk at the wind's edge,
feel its sharp teeth
tearing thin strips of flesh
to lie on the drift
of pebbles on the shore.

The way of the wind
drags at my mind's edge,
tearing thin strips
from the slough of my brain
to lie on the shift
of seaweed on the rocks.

My face to the sea
I walk at the world's edge,
feel each new wave
tearing thin strips of thought
to bandage my heart
cut off by the tide.

The Treadmill of Fret

Worry and fear, your two familiars,
walk always beside you
matching their step to yours,
certain you never can escape
their joint dictatorship.

To break the pattern they impose,
the treadmill of fret,
quicken your step,
push them behind
to whistle to heel and bind.

Use worry's grit to hone your thought,
give keenness to your brain,
with fear as taper set alight
imagination's wild delight
and learn to live again.

Heart's Weight

Is this man heavy?—
only my heart's weight,
makes him light
in the deft reachings of the night,
heavy when break of day
hardens the cold wet clay
of settled flight
to ending of our brief delight.

Is this man heavy?—
only the weight of grief
nagging beyond belief
at bruised rib-cageing,
a hardening and ageing
of major artery,
no makeshift surgery
can bring relief.

Is this man heavy?—
fixed in an abstract stare
knotted in strings of care
only to pain aware,
as lying underground
fast in my bride-shroud bound
making no move or sound
I wait his weight.

Viewpoint

We are both a bit obsessed
by my graveyard
and the disturbing view
of tombstones seen
through cottage window panes,
especially those two
so stiff and straight,
stark sentinels of time
upstanding for the Queen
in some old nursery rhyme.

We are both a bit obsessed
by solitude
and the distracting view
of commerce seen
through narrow winding lanes;
people on business bent
are models used
in window drawing class,
a pattern of intent
we breathe upon the glass.

We are both a bit obsessed
by fantasy
and the diverting view
of life-span seen
through mirror'd window panes,
a world of outside in
and inside out,
in which two tombstones move
beyond the bounds of time
and in and out of love.

Searchlight

Moonlight is clinical
searching without compassion
for the ills of day,
winkling them out to writhe
on microscopic glass
throughout the night.

Daylight is savagery,
the sun's rays tiger-striped
to claw the heart and burn
what's left to drifting ash,
a bone-white powder blown
on heat of noon.

Dusk is more circumspect;
the fires of day damped down
the moon not yet in sight,
unfretted by the light
the heart takes brief respite
before the night.

Sunday Train

Between stations there is no light,
no notion of travelling to arrive
by a recognised route, only blackness
and a slow circling of unspecified places.
Re-routed, we are adrift on a sea of uncertainty
and wonder idly if a sense of purpose
should so easily be lost
or if it is reasonable to want to know
the exact time and place of our arrival.

An Asian woman talks incessantly
and a stream of words divides the carriage;
on this side we read or sleep
and a young man, stoned,
out of his mind inside his earphones
moves his lips to a pattern of his own choosing.

The air is sour with age, and a smell of soot
clings to the windows; outside
an excessively English Sunday moves
beyond our reach, and we are moved to talk
about the pattern of the past
and the time when we were all too certain
of the horrors we were about
and of where we feared to arrive.

Suddenly a station looms, and now
there is only hope in the future . . .

                    (Remembrance Sunday, November 1987)

Walled Garden

for Maureen Hennessy

Your roses spill bright petals on the ground
I pick them to augment my pot-pourri,
kicking hard first-fall apples from my path
thumb testing flesh of those still on the tree,
rifling your neighbour's purple-breasted plums
and waiting for the globus pink-tinged quince
to ripen to authentic marmalade,
too rarified for bed and breakfast use.

The coolness of a leaf-green canopy
encompasses your garden in the heat,
we sit in the oasis of its shade
and revel in the fragrance all around.
On a stone bench you strip your honesty
with Hera watching slyly from behind,
idly you rock the hammock with your foot
and trail your hand in matted undergrowth.

Indoors you keep an ever open house
dispensing tea from round black-bellied pot
to visitors arriving day or night.
Unwinding ravelled threads of people's lives
you listen with compassion undismayed
to tales of intrigue or a schoolgirl's plight
but keep that walled-in garden undisclosed,
a fragment of yourself inviolate.

The Ballad of Brighton Beach

It was when we moved down to the seaside
Dad still had some money to burn,
he invented what he called the Sand Game
and played it with each girl in turn.

He didn't hoard vulgar postcards
or boast of his one-night stands,
just collected little glass bottles
of different coloured sands.

One was marked *Shanklin with Susan*
and one labelled *Letty in Lyme*,
and each had been worn in her navel
for a teasing fraction of time.

He tried every colour with Sally,
who lasted for nearly a week,
and mixed up his sands in a cocktail
till she called him a naughty old freak.

He'd hidden his store of sand bottles
in a cupboard well out of my sight,
but I knew where to find what I wanted
when I raided his room in the night.

The best of his varied collection
was *Sophie of San Tropez*,
but I settled for *Betty from Brighton*
which suited my ploy for the day.

I wanted to tease my new boy-friend
as we lay in our favourite place,
to get him to try out the Sand Game
and savour the look on his face.

I put on my briefest bikini
as bait in my amorous trap,
though I hadn't reckoned to love him
till he laid his head in my lap.

He trickled the sand in my navel
and found me a Venus shell,
it was tiny and fragile and perfect
and he said that it suited me well.

So we played at the Sand Game together
till our measure of time ran red,
the blood in my veins sang glory
and the beach was our marriage bed.

Catch a Snowflake if You Can

a poem for children, in memory of Penny Gee

Catch a snowflake if you can
see the patterns as they run
hold them melting in your hand
lick your fingers as they numb.

Try to find an icicle
put it in the microwave,
watch it turn into a pool
which the buzzer cannot save.

Nothing is quite what it seems
living is for here and now,
so defrost your frozen dreams
do not wait to question how.

Hold your hands out to the wind
let the rain run down your face,
step in every fairy ring
hide in each enchanted place.

Write your words upon the air
see them curve and rhyme and scan,
make new patterns everywhere
catch a snowflake if you can.

A Question of Carelessness

Can one lose people
as one loses things,
by being careless
or forgetful of the press
of their own needs,

a sense of loss most keen
and finger-tips most sore
when scrabbling on the floor
sifting the dust to find
torn pieces of the pattern of the mind?

Only for that short time
it takes to catch a breath
and think about the death
of what we love the most,
and lose all hope

then, surging on a tide
of love and pain,
sure as the round world spins
people like misplaced pins
turn up to prick again!

Rude Awakening: a night-owl's lament

for Frances Cole

A curling feather from night's pillowed deep
floats on the edge of day to feel the wind,
the mind's slow pulling from the edge of sleep
arrested midway, threatens to rescind.

Day's growing credence like a creaking cart
trundles across the brain dispersing night,
lodges a first enchantment in the heart
and puts a late last dream to scuttling flight.

Long fingers of the night reach out to find
fresh channels in the unresponding grey,
enticing images invade the mind
and winkle out resistance to the day.

My thoughts run rampant as a flag unfurled
untimely bold, I wake to face the world.

Kitchen Cantata

for Creina Francis

A kitchen is a sensuous delight
on which imagination's eye is fed,
rows of glass jars, their contents jewel-bright,
saffron near-gold, pepper paprika red,
mustard soft yellow as old pinchbeck sheen;
then various textures temptingly displayed:
hard crunch of grain—rice, pasta, soya bean,
soft drift of flour waiting to be weighed.

Huge Spanish onions hanging from a string,
a set of copper pans, an ordered row,
as finely polished as a girl's first ring,
well-scrubbed pine table, stoneware jugs and bowl
piled high with fruit, the smell of home-made bread,
without all these a kitchen's heart is dead.

A Day by the Sea

for Lorraine Curtis

The day's too dull for pocket cameras,
their quick impressions of the changing scene,
and I've no skill with crayons or with paints
to catch the colours of the grey-green sea,
but what a picture's painted in my head
of surf-tossed kelpies racing for the shore,
risking their necks each time they reach the rocks
recovering, to race on as before
only to break their backs upon the cliffs.

The off-white seagulls skirl across the sky
drift with the wind and follow on the tide;
intent on fishing now they seem to cry:
come back, come back, come back and see us play,
the sea is here for ever, not one day.

Buttons

for Cynthia Hawkins

Buttons are lying all around the house
on every surface flat enough to hold
assorted faces in precise array:
the opalescent glimmering of shell,
little Satsuma pansies from Japan
and silver flowers on exquisite jade,
cloisonné pinpoints of enamelled blue,
Victorian messages in jewelled gold
and mourning circles with the gleam of jet,
old Roman coins and Persian turquoises
and, poignant with the memory of war,
a tiny compass from a button's heart;
while in between these relics of past trust
bright butterflies are dancing in the dust.

The Icing on the Cake

You read to me on the 'phone
in a voice clear as a tenor bell
but more beautiful,
and in an instant I was transported
East of the Sun and West of the Moon
to the magic kingdom of my childhood,
where innocence was safe for a hundred years,
curiosity not a carnal sin
and patience and love
always rewarded in the end.

The beauty of the story moved us both
and, anxious not to dissect or desiccate
the perfection of understanding
that lies like new snowflakes
on our memories,
I resisted the impulse to tell you my thoughts
and busied my hands with homeliness,
baking a cake with flakes of coconut
good enough to eat, or to keep
iced and decorated, on a shelf
in the museum of childhood,
where it lies
beside the tray the packmen used
to show their wares,
peddling not books but custard tarts
and penny buns covered with coconut,
that we called snowballs.

Pot-Pourri

You just touch the 't'
with your tongue,
you said,
as you asked me
to make pot-pourri
and I—who had never
been able to touch flower petals
without a shudder—
picked up the fallen bounty
from stone flags,
shook two blowsy heads
into a white bowl
and looked in an old herbal
for a recipe for pot-pourri.

No recipe
only instructions for distilling
the essence of the rose
to make a cordial
for the relief of vomittings,
a powerful remedy
against the flux.

I can understand
that for you
it may be the essence
of God's goodness
that he spare you
the burden of infinity,
but for me
it is the distillation of divinity
that there should be roses beyond time
and time for pot-pourri.

Book of Hours

Petals I picked from flowers in full bloom
spread out in valanced dark beneath my bed
give lasting fragrance in an empty room,
their brilliance drying to a dusky red
empurpled lavender and tawny gold;
such cloistered colour should not smell so sweet
nor glow so strangely being sere and old
and crisply wrinkled with remembered heat.

But beauty can be obdurate and strange
and memory wither slowly in old age,
its warmth encapsulated on a page
of some illuminated Book of Hours,
whose jewelled offices as brightly range
as mine do hourly when I turn my flowers.

Door-stop

Door-stop of white quartz,
shutting experience out
or keeping it in?
All that rough imagery
worn to hand-warmed smoothness.

I have seen children
behind the glass of years
wearing my childhood's clothes,
their too-bright eyes
unfocussed on my books,
their wax fingers
playing with my toys.

Unspoken words
alert my inner ear;
I reach towards
the perfect painted egg
my daughter brings me
every Easter Day,
her cupped hands cradling love.

She fills my silence
with her chatter-song
and joy irradiates
the lovely oval
of her unborn face.

Time's Mantle

'Those ladies at their looms! What
is to become of us? . . .

I wear time's mantle
and they will not reach me beyond
the midnight crossing . . .'

(from *The Word Mantle*, by Kevin Crossley-Holland)

I wear time's mantle, smiling
as my thoughts of Spring
quicken the breathing,
sweeten the breath, and
leave the smell of death
no space to cling.

I wrap it round me, flaunting
the cut and the fit,
over-large stitches
concealed in deep pleat,
bright patchwork pieces
appliquéd with spit.

I wear it fondly, schooling
the lolloping horse
of my childhood's course,
pushing and pulling,
my rag-bag of days
rummaged for praise.

Theatre in the Round

Artists paint light which colours what they see
and sculptors coax dimension out of stone,
poets carve meaning from their new-found words
to scratch fresh patterns on primeval bone.

True beauty has an ever-changing face
and vision is a theatre in the round,
perception is essential to all thought
but what we see is simply what we've found.

We know there's nothing new beneath the sun
and space was animated from the start,
though colour, shape and texture please the eye
new ways of seeing activate the heart.

I rattle up my slatted window-blind
astonished as the sunlight floods my mind.

Foster Child

for Cynthia Senior

A few days old, you lie in my arms
plucking in low-key demand
the heart-strings of my barrenness
with your small sucking noises of reproach.

I dare not offer too much in response,
negate the bravery your natural mother showed
when she consigned you to a chain of care
that will not stop at me,
but I can claim the natural right of prayer
and hold you at my breast to suckle strength
from that great body of concern
which is your new-found family.

The Wake

a poem in memory of Natalie Winslow

The table was laid ready for your wake
when we arrived
two tall black candlesticks as for a bier,
a meal kept hot,
a row of glasses and the opened wine
cooling on ice.

We drank to you, wished you safe journey and
a last God-speed
then turned to talk of poems we had brought,
how some had worked
some not, when inspiration in the mind
could not find words.

We had no words—for all our chiselled verse—
to tell out grief,
hedged carefully around the subject, spoke
with you in mind;
it was your vividness and caustic wit
sustained our talk.

Landscape Painting

Long lilting lines of hills
gentle the distance,
ribbons of red brick
make criss-cross patterns
and a gap-toothed hedge
straggles across the foreground
like a frame uncertain of its purpose.

Travelling by train
great swathes of landscape
obtrude on the imagination
till the eye, normally obsessed by print,
is forced instead to rest upon the view:
those muddy browns and greys
and the bright splash
of that incredibly fresh green
which is the English spring personified.

I think of last evening
and the room we sat in
peopled with landscapes
and one lovely nude
walking away,
a full-length figure of a girl
the flesh tones vibrant and compassionate.

I think of how a man's life
danced upon the screen
and I remember
earlier in the week
walking in Lowry landscapes
in the street,
his stick-like figures
crowding on the mind.

A man obsessed by loneliness
he painted crowds
that scurried to and fro
and left him there,
a lone observer
of their eccentricity.

I watch my fellow travellers
and my thoughts run on
into the landscape . . .

An Unrhymed Sonnet

for Janet

A late Spring evening, and the sea-green light
just disappearing from a darkening sky
behind your tree, its unleaved branches still
as delicately wrought as filigree
but black not silver. One faint star the first
to glimmer softly in the growing dusk
then suddenly the dog-star, hard and bright,
its diamond brilliance heralding the dark.

You paint suburban landscapes with a brush
dipped in discernment and your artist's eye
watches the shifting patterns with delight;
the tree and sky, roof-tops and hedge are all
part of your scene, material for your art,
as much your medium as the paints you use.

The Water Park

a painting for Janet

Reflections of an opalescent sky,
its steely blue chasing the sun's last streaks
of flame-red warmth into the winter grass,
a flock of white tern keening overhead
or forming diamond patterns on the lake,
two hoodie crows, black and malevolent
hunched high up on the fence presaging doom
as though they knew the scene demanded it;
a man-made lake beside the Mersey Bank
a few feet from the new-built motorway
and noisy excavations for a bridge
the far side of the fence.

We keep this side
watching a bright-haired boy jump up and down
a pile of rough-hewn elms, lifting his feet
with unremitting energy and zest.
Remembering when I last jumped for joy
I flex my fingers, chilled inside my gloves,
and walk on down the leaf-encrusted path
dodging the children playing Robin Hood,
the anglers ankle-deep in Mersey mud,
back to the certainty of scones and tea
and home-made parkin to keep out the cold
that creeps indoors as Bonfire Night draws near.

The Last Curtain

on a painting by Frank Spears

His painted lips are dry with age,
white face a mask now death is near;
agility all skin and bone,
the feet that skipped are cold as fear
the juggling hands like sculptured stone.

No craftsman's concept nor no fool's
deflects his inward-looking view,
no memory of circus light
illuminates the world he knew
or magnifies his failing sight.

You painted his last curtain, and
you finished it just weeks before
the night you threw your brushes down
enraged that you could paint no more;
immaculate and sad-eyed clown

you rang your own last curtain down.

A Perfumed Candle

A daỹ of wine and roses, and of trust
both given and received amongst old friends
though two of them at best have no life left
to savour or to share, except their fears.
My mind fills up with sadness as the warmth
fades from the scene and leaves an acrid smell
of burnt-out intellect and memory.

I light a perfumed candle which soon burns
a lambent circle in its oval tin,
the surface glimmers in the growing dark.
I look into the light until my thoughts,
never remote from you, curl round the flame
in search of comfort for my grief and yours,
assuaging conscience and the fret of pain.

Perspective

Children draw houses flat upon the page,
square windows sightless eyes for seeing through;
perspective is a thing that comes with age
and they see homes as houses with no view.

Lovers draw houses solid with intent,
wide windows they can see their children through;
such rosy-petalled futures they present,
life's pattern ever fresh and ever new.

The aged and the lonely live inside
the sightless houses they as children drew;
the petals fallen from the flowers that died,
they wonder sadly why they have no view.

The Visit

for Physhe Wright

'... How can I let you go,
     you that I worship so? ...'

'He sang an old song
from the hey-day of his youth
to us and a bewildered audience
fidgeting, not in the stalls
but in their comfortable garden chairs.

The old woman shuffling past
stopped to direct
a vituperative glance
at our accord
and scatter curses on his untrimmed beard.

She has forgotten
how the sight of him
could so completely carry her away
that she left husband, home and children
for his sake.

Behind them a whirligig
blows wetly in the wind,
clean knickers, sheets and towels all proclaim
a silent testimony
to their failing powers.

Dream Sequence

(written after a heart attack)

Snow turned to white paint
inside the bath, and turned again
to puzzlement and pain;
a scent of honeysuckle weighing on the air
deepened to purple and a shadowed bruise
that spread across my face . . .

Innocent as children
hiding in the big bed
we clung together,
till voices in the hall below
warned of discovery
and you disappeared.

I found myself outside another room—
a Bluebeard's chamber not yet stained with blood—
half turned the door-knob,
listened at the door,
then left the rightful inmate undisturbed
and came away to search the house for you.

Finding the bathroom, and you
incongruously asleep there
stretched on a divan,
I washed my hands,
kissed you 'Goodbye' and left
walking slowly down a long flight of stairs . . .

This whiteness clouds my vision
and I cannot see,
see if my hands are clean;
the face in the glass is white
and all my shadowed bruises look like dirt
that will not wash away.

Decaffeinated

for Brian Doney

Decaffeinated living is too bland
for those of us who like our flavours sharp
and drifting with the tide has no appeal
to swimmers who love battling for the shore;
ignoring easy paths around our feet
while straining for a sight of distant hills,
we take our pleasures hardly and deny
the heart's increasing need for quietude.

Days knitted on thin needles are too taut
for variegated patterns to emerge,
better to make myself a comfort scarf
from fabric loosely woven in the mind
than ravel custom's stitches row on row—
good knitters check their tension as they go—
slowly, not feebly, is the way to live
as, feeble, I would rate myself half dead.

Better Blind?

Perhaps it will be better
when I'm blind;
people will start to practise
being kind,
read me their poetry,
fetch me a chair,
help me to find the things I cannot see
and mop my spillage when I drink my tea.

Blindness could be
a strange relief,
people might understand my disability
accept I couldn't see,
instead of being in a state
of constant irritation
with my tiresome inability
to hear their brave attempts at conversation.

Self-pity is a loathsome state of mind;
shut out, cut off
from real communication,
only aware sometimes of altercation—
for people raise their voices when they're cross—
I cloak my angry wretchedness with comfort:
they may not have much patience with my deafness
but it could be much better when I'm blind.

Serenity

So this is the serenity of age
anticipated from my earliest youth
and sought through constant winnowing of truth,
this effervescence of emotion sprayed
as from a fountain playing all day long
first up, then down, now fast and then too slow—
impossible to tell which way to go
when winds of change blow everywhere as strong.

Not even adolescence made me burn
like this tempestuous swing from high to low,
from doubt to faith, and the desire to learn
conflicting with the arrogant 'I know'—
I reach behind me, wipe my childhood slate,
tell all to God and then sit down to wait.

Elder

The elder flowers
outside my window,
filigree in moonlight
are white as snow blossom
in the untimely cold
of a summer night.

I remember now
June in Grindelwald,
sun, shining on the roofs
and on the pink cherry,
snow, bright on the mountains
and on the high paths.

Wakened by cowbells
outside our window
and a young man who played
his ringing Alpenhorn,
we walked before breakfast up to the Schwarzhorn.

Meadows were alight
flowers yellow, pink
and deep blue of gentian;
the freshness of their scent
still clinging to our hands,
we reached the pension.

I draw my curtains,
elder is not bold,
drifting fragrance drowns
in remembered sweetness.
So many summers since,
must this one, here, be cold?

Shelves in the Mind

Shelves in the mind hold past experience
row upon row like once familiar books,
their pages, thumbed, open at random now.
My neighbour plants her thyme, I dig mine up:
hers is a secret store of future scent,
mine has the pungent smell of memory.

The trim lavender of my common-sense
hedges me round, roses drop petals
for my pot-pourri and wine-red clematis
scales my flint wall. The pages of my books
breathe out the past and random browsing stirs
the fragrant dust, but you and I, my love,
have free exchange each of the other's mind
and Figsbury Ring was Striding Edge to-day.
Where the round sweep of Downs, stretched out below,
gave space for far-flung thought, you walked with me
the safe side of the firing range's fence
and carefully I matched my steps to yours.

The hurt of your long absence festers still
and still I search for soothing antidote;
herbs are for healing, may experience lend
greenness of touch to fingers stiff with age,
that pricked-out seedlings of my thyme may grow
to ease the dragging sore that will not mend.

Memorabilia

The small memorabilia of the heart
are central to the pattern of each day,
abiding certainties that light our way
infusing order into muddled thought.

The secret galleries of mind can hold
a crowd of images like pictures stored,
their muted colours are a miser's hoard
an inner treasury to count as gold.

As flowers gathered in a lifetime's trust
glow with new beauty in remembered light,
so tissued layers of dream enhance the night
with shaken clouds of rainbow-coloured dust.

Age has no pleasure youth can comprehend
but dreams in age are joy that has no end.

Records

for Stephen Stuart-Smith

Searching old records for the ones to keep
successive lives are crumbled into dust,
there were so may deaths, why can't I trust
each night's dissembling death that leads to sleep.

Re-reading volumes for the missing sheet
no option but to sort the dusty shelves,
replace the layers of discarded selves
and listen for the needle's thin repeat.

The mind smoothes out the brown-stained folds of time
the gaps between lend meaning to the words,
my heart responds in harmonising thirds
and music long unheard provokes new rhyme.

How like a hooky rug a life can seem,
in trust renewed I watch as colours gleam.

The Bishops' Road to Winchester

Nothing should hurt like this in absence from
the rugged landscape that I still call home
except the still raw wound that absence caused,
but ah these trees, so savagely destroyed,
knock at my heart for pity and for pain.

Their ravaged roots bleached white with downland chalk
once splendid trunks a road block, nothing more,
they sprawl across the scene they lately crowned;
piles of cut timber lying on the ground
shout their reproach to every passer-by.

This road is steep with history and pride
a Roman highway, later used by kings
and strewn with pennies when a bishop died,
scored with deep tracks by mediæval sledge
that carried timber, dated now by rings.

In abdication of their kingship here
these trees compel my homage and my tears.

Harlequinade

A half moon and a striped balloon
in apron shades of white and blue
float banners in the sky too soon
above the empty barbecue.
Too soon for dreams, too soon to weep,
too soon to wish the world away,
too soon to let the need for sleep
give night ascendance over day.

The churchyard cat, pearl grey, hunts mice
in fitful spurts of energy,
I know that fear exacts its price
and watch in careful apathy
the weaving movements in the grass
and round King Alfred's dubious stone,
till all the lurking shadows pass
and I again lie here alone.

A black and yellow domino
plays Romeo in the moon-bright lane,
a single crimson beanstalk rose
nudges his Juliet's window pane.
Too late his feet begin their climb
to pluck the rose and blunt the thorn,
too late the pattern of their mime
unfolds its silence on the dawn.

Cornus Norman Hadden

My first love affair with a tree:
Cornus Norman Hadden—
an unlikely name
for that close-packed mass of flowers,
flat-growing, open to the sun
on delicate slender branches,
whose pale-green frills are
layered like Victorian petticoats—
first seen in June
bridal whiteness only faintly flushed.

I wanted to touch
to stroke the petals
and lay my face on their smooth cushions,
but I just stood there
open-mouthed and stupid
in my adoration.

By mid-July
petals, less thickly spaced
more fully flushed,
dropped as I watched
making no sound, but each one
dry and brown-veined
soon as it touched the ground.
I scooped them in my hands
and tried to weep
for such short-lived perfection,
but I just knelt there
dry-mouthed and stupid
in my grief.

Country Lore

Ripe elderberries turn their tassels down
as token they have juice enough for wine,
while russet cider apples press to brown
and grapes hang darkly purple on the vine.

Fennel and rue together make good sack,
their honeyed sweetness works to golden balm,
ripe bramble clusters change from red to black
and scarlet rowan wards off witchcraft's harm.

All nature ripens in a mellow glow,
mankind alone matures to sober white:
my scarlet tassels make unseemly show
O, rowan, save me from the witches' spite.

Garden Lore

Not quite a witch but something near akin
I pick rose-petals for my pot-pourri,
consigning black fly to an instant death;
I dead head pansies for their growing good,
talk to my Twickle Purple lavender,
feed struggling sweet peas with a strange rich juice,
steep elderflowers for home-brewed champagne
and chop the spreading mint to use in pies.

Such industry should have more just reward:
this grower's fingers are not green but black
and all my witch's lore is learned from books;
spells, second-hand, are sometimes slow to work
and borrowed remedies not always safe,
my plants need most protection from myself.
Yet as I watch the colours glow and spread
I scatter love on everything that grows.

Pressed Flowers

An afternoon of bluebells in the wood,
the shimmer of a thousand calendars
reaching and reaching into distant haze,
evoking memories of childhood jars
crammed with huge bunches carried proudly home,
and armfuls of wild garlic left outside,
too pungent for a dressing-up bouquet.

Those flowers we picked for pressing long ago
are growing now around our tired feet:
soft yellow primroses, sweet violets
that once were shy, now rampant in the grass,
spurge, like new pennies on their long green stalks
small star-shaped celandines, and windflowers,
the fragile drift of wood anemones.

I tried in vain to lift a windflower root
and picked some violets for old time's sake,
knowing full well they will not last till night.
Remembered strictures ringing in my head
I hid the bunch behind my back in guilt:
I looked and looked on pictures of the past
and carried armfuls of wild memory home.

Shifting Sand

Look forward or look back, it's much the same
the corridors of years stretch out in line,
their rows of doors, conjecture or surmise,
intriguingly half open in the mind.

Acceptance of mortality's short span
can sharpen up the focus of the light,
a hair-line crevice in the shell of time
give breadth of vision to the questing sight.

The discipline of concentrated thought
finds buried treasure under shifting sand
and moments of bright intuition know
the how and why that other people planned.

Experiencing the thinking of the past
can deepen salient colours of today,
the painting of a landscape of a life
intensified because it's in a frame.

Passiflora

The heat of summer faded
so I lit my fire,
brought candles, wine and peaches,
piled red love apples in a cut glass bowl
and set two brilliant passion flowers to flaunt
their purple filaments as centrepiece.

We ate and drank together
but the sun had gone
and high between us rose a wall of glass,
cold, hard and as impenetrable
as though each could not see
the flames still leaping on the other side.

I kicked against the glass
until it broke
then washed the splinters from my blinded eyes
to see the flowers folding on the night;
bleak daylight will take over with love gone,
familiar order turned to a new wall.

August in Durham

Cream teas served in the crypt to chatterers
and women walking on St Cuthbert's shrine,
the verger leads a stand-in choir to place,
his chewing sends a shiver down my spine.
Outside the grass is lush on Palace Green
and we've just sung the rousing ninetieth psalm;
our days are numbered in the sight of God
who shields us everlastingly from harm.
My eye accepts that nothing is unchanged
and I'm a tourist in a foreign place,
my heart defies the changes and responds
to the eternal steadfastness of grace.

An old enchantment holds me as I walk
slowly around my birthright, feel that grace
streams from the circling hills to guide my feet,
the heady air blows fresh against my face
and water—nowhere else as good to drink—
lays silken benediction on my skin.
Found music fills my heart to call me home
and not to listen almost seems a sin
but reason gathers strongly in my head,
a backward step in age is foolishness,
accepting change both here and in myself
leaves me with greater loyalty, not less.

Autumn

I who remember days of warm delight
now watch the turning hours with anxious eyes,
hiding my dried rose-petals out of sight,
grieving for summer's vanished butterflies.

The last thin sliver of a waning moon
accentuates the dying of the year,
the scuffed-up leaves go thin and dry too soon
and drift against the empty chalet door.

Yet autumn's vibrant colours lift the mind
beyond such thoughts of ageing and decay,
lie fallow with me, sweetheart, till we find
encroaching darkness bursting into day.

Full Circle

A thousand images have changed their shape,
old words have found new meaning in themselves,
since first I threw my apples in your path
and you ran eagerly to gather them.

My apples, scarlet once, are golden now
and rolling still to your defenceless feet;
you fend them off, then stoop to lift and throw
till perfect circles pass and, bruising, meet.

So to and fro the bitter-sweetness rides,
we barter verse across the gap of years;
apples improve with keeping, as do words,
their juices linger on the tongue like tears.

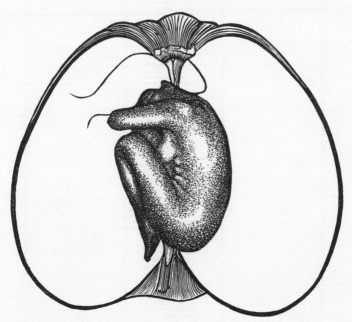

Nude in an Apple: wood engraving © Graham Williams